A Gift

For:

From:

Napoleon Dynamite™

HOW TO IMPROVE YOUR SKILLS SO YOU DON'T LOOK LIKE AN IDIOT

GIFT BOOKS
from Hallmark

BOK 2083

Andrews McMeel
Publishing, LLC

This edition published in 2007 by Andrews McMeel Publishing, LLC,
exclusively for Hallmark Cards, Inc.

ISBN: 0-7407-7226-0

www.hallmark.com

Edited by Bob Elser
Cover and Book Design by Eric Schotland

www.andrewsmcmeel.com

CONTENTS

Introduction 7

Job Hunting Skills 8

Workplace Skills 16

Interpersonal Skills 24

Grooming Skills 32

Dating Skills 40

Shopping Skills 48

Guys Only Skills 54

Girls Only Skills 68

6

It's good to have skills. Skills can pretty much keep you from looking like an idiot. How many times have you seen someone goof something up and then you go, "What an idiot." The last thing you want is for people to be saying "idiot" about you. So learn the following skills and you'll pretty much be the best that you can be. Heck, you might even be better than that.

7

JOB HUNTING
SKILLS

When the interviewer asks what kind of experience you have, just tell 'em you have **quick hands** and **feet,** and you'll probably get the job.

8

JOB HUNTING SKILLS

10

Always bring a snack to your interview. It shows that you can take care of yourself and that you're not just looking for a free lunch.

Tell the interviewer **right up front**
that you're willing to do **whatever**
it takes to get the job done,
but no one **ever means that**
so don't worry about it
when you get the job.

13

Bring a pad of paper and a pencil to all interviews and pretend to write stuff down.

You don't really have to write it down — just go along with it until it's time to tour the facility.

WORKPLACE SKILLS

Sooner or later, someone is going to ask you to explain something by

16   drawing them a picture.

Like, "Hey, I don't get it. You're going to

have to draw me a picture." So go ahead

and draw them a picture of a

Labracougar.

That ought to shut them up for awhile.

once you get a job, right away

learn what side your bread

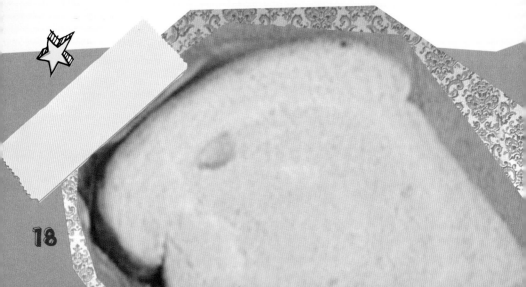

18

is buttered on.
Butter is the success
you can always
count on.

19

WORK PLACE
SKILLS

Never be afraid to **COPY** famous writers and artists. Some of the greatest of all-time copied a certain style and pretended not to notice until they got paid.

27

 **TIP:** Don't use colored ink to send memos.

It'll make you look like an idiot and your fame will go right out the window.

INTERPERSONAL
SKILLS

Always make eye contact, unless you don't want to, then just **bend over** and make a **groaning noise.**

AIR SERVICES INTERNATIONAL

TIME MACHINE MODULUS

POWER

HIGH
ON

25

INTERPERSONAL
SKILLS

It's okay to make up stories about your past to create a life of **mystery,**

because hey, that's the way it's always been done.

27

INTERPERSONAL
SKILLS

When you meet an adult,

always use "sir" and "ma'am."

Now, if their last name _is_ Ma'am, then just say Mr. Ma'am or Mrs. Ma'am – and be done with it.

29

INTERPERSONAL
SKILLS

Learn one good dance move.

You gotta have a one-of-a-kind dance move. And make sure it's got a twirl in it.

Like, step, step, slide. . . twirl.

SWEET!

GROOMING
SKILLS

Never wear a T-shirt with the same picture on it two days in a row, but jeesh, who would do that, anyway!

GROOMING SKILLS

34

You can always connect the freckles on your face with an ink pen and hope you make a constellation. That'll be a different look.

GROOMING SKILLS

Learn to take care of
your eyebrows.

Brush in an east-to-west direction,
not north-to-south.

37

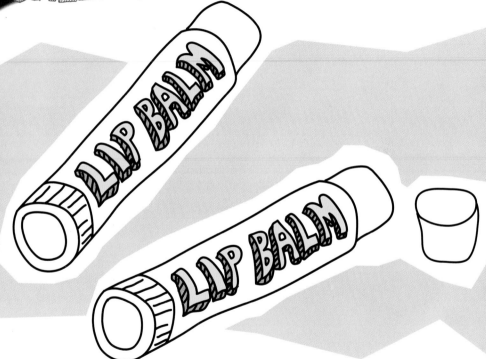

Carry a stick of lip balm, plus a back-up stick, because in most societies cracked lips are a sure sign of weakness.

DATING SKILLS

If you want to let

someone know you like them,

offer them a Nugget of Friendship,

then see where it goes from there.

If you see any food stuck in your date's teeth, it's okay to tell them

if you use Pig Latin

(hav-ay food-ay in your tooth-ay).

If they don't get it, you've done all you can do.

43

A slice of whole-wheat bread works great if you want to practice kissing.

Plus, when practice is over, you've got yourself a nutritious snack.

Here's a **sure-fire** way to impress your dates.

Take them to a food court and simply say,

"Go ahead and order the foot-long,

I can afford it."

SHOPPING SKILLS

Here's something you should know about grocery stores. They always put the expensive food up high because **tall people** are used to **reaching their goals.**

VOTE
FOR
PEDRO

49

SHOPPING SKILLS

Don't waste your money on foreign products.

Like, take **cheese.** Expensive cheese

doesn't come from the cream of

more expensive cows.

50

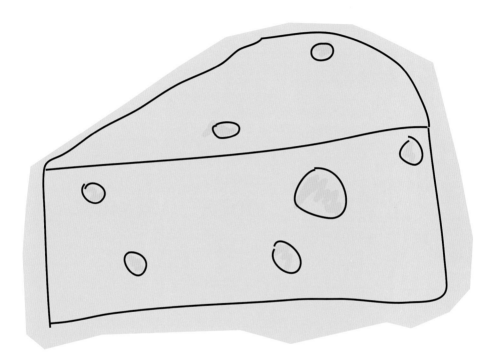

All cows cost about the same.

SHOPPING SKILLS

You can find some great bargains
in second-hand stores.

And whoever says you can't wear plaid
with plaid has never been to Scotland.

GUYS ONLY

SKILLS

Learn to tie your own tie so you never have to wear a clip-on. Clip-ons are for rodeo clowns.

Make some sweet moola.

Girls like guys who make

some sweet moola.

Learn how to polish your shoes so they don't look scuffed. Girls will think you're a foot-dragger and nothing good will ever come out of a bunch of girls thinking that.

SHOE POLISH

FLIPPERIN' SWEET

SHOE POLISH

59

With practice, you can break out of

almost any headlock by shouting,

"Get offa me," followed by a cool

twist-and-shove move.

SKILLS

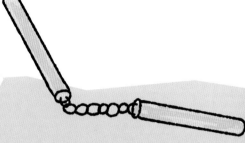

When facing a dangerous situation,
make a whirling motion with your hands
to create a barrier of **invincibility**
and **protection.**

Never walk with your

hands in your pockets because if

you have to perform an **immediate**

spin move to avoid danger, you'll probably

fall down and end up

64

getting eaten alive.

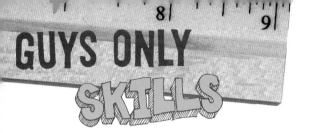
If you find yourself getting beat up

for no good reason, go ahead and

just play dead. It might save you

some time.

GIRLS ONLY

SKILLS

Act like you have all the answers.

No one will be that surprised.

Napoleon Dynamite

ANSWERS

Try to go through each day with a song in your heart, a bounce in your step,

and a **snappy retort** in your head, like—

Learn to tease your hair.

Any hair that's worth its salt should be able to **take a joke**, otherwise, it's just a bunch of limp protein hanging around.

Occasionally wear **big, puffy sleeves**

because it will make you feel like a princess.

And feeling like a princess is second only

to feeling like the Queen of

the Wolverines.

74

75

Glance, don't stare.

The googly-eyed look

will only attract the wrong species.

Here's a flirting tip.

Playfully bite your lip,

then look down. But not too hard, because a

flesh wound takes all the fun out of it.

79

A LIFETIME SKILL

Heck, do whatever you want, because you feel like doing whatever you want.

Gosh!